NIGHTMARES

POEMS TO TROUBLE YOUR SLEEP

by **JACK PRELUTSKY**

illustrated by **ARNOLD LOBEL**

GREENWILLOW BOOKS

A Division of William Morrow & Company, Inc., New York

4 5

Library of Congress Cataloging in Publication Data
Prelutsky, Jack. Nightmares. Summary: Twelve poems featuring a vampire, were-
wolf, ghoul, and other monsters.   1. Monsters—Juvenile poetry. [1. Monsters—
Poetry]   I.   Lobel, Arnold.   II.   Title.   PZ8.3.P9Ni   811'.5'4   76-4820
ISBN 0-688-80053-X   ISBN 0-688-84053-1 lib. bdg.

For Arnold

CONTENTS

THE HAUNTED HOUSE

On a hilltop bleak and bare
   looms the castle of despair,
only phantoms linger there
within its dismal walls.
Through the dark they're creeping, crawling,
frenzied furies battling, brawling,
sprawling, calling, caterwauling
through the dusky halls.

Filmy visions, ever flocking,
dart through chambers, crudely mocking,
rudely rapping, tapping, knocking
on the crumbling doors.
Tortured spirits whine and wail,
they grope and grasp, they wildly flail,
their hollow voices rasp and rail
beneath the moldering floors.

Shadows from the dim hereafter
hang from every creaking rafter,
laughing disembodied laughter
in their ghostly glee.
Shades of evanescent matter
whisper their unearthly patter,
rattle chains that chill and shatter
on their spectral spree.

Revenants on misty perches
taunt the ghost that lunges, lurches
as it desperately searches
for its vanished head.
Shapeless wraiths devoid of feeling
hover blindly by the ceiling
ranting, chanting, shrieking, squealing
promises of dread.

In the corners, eyes are gleaming,
everywhere are nightmares streaming,
diabolic horrors screaming
in the sombrous air.
So shun this place where specters soar—
it's you and you they're waiting for
to haunt your souls forevermore
in their castle of despair.

THE WILL O' THE WISP

You are lost in the desolate forest
where the stars give a pitiful light,
but the faraway glow of the will o' the wisp
offers hope in the menacing night.

It is lonely and cold in the forest
and you shiver with fear in the damp,
as you follow the way of the will o' the wisp
and the dance of its flickering lamp.

But know as you trudge through the forest
toward that glistering torch in the gloom
that the eerie allure of the will o' the wisp
summons you down to your doom.

It will lead you astray in the forest
over ways never traveled before.
If ever you follow the will o' the wisp
you'll never be seen anymore.

THE BOGEYMAN

In the desolate depths of a perilous place
the bogeyman lurks, with a snarl on his face.
Never dare, never dare to approach his dark lair
for he's waiting . . . just waiting . . . to get you.

He skulks in the shadows, relentless and wild
in his search for a tender, delectable child.
With his steely sharp claws and his slavering jaws
oh he's waiting . . . just waiting . . . to get you.

Many have entered his dreary domain
but not even one has been heard from again.
They no doubt made a feast for the butchering beast
and he's waiting . . . just waiting . . . to get you.

In that sulphurous, sunless and sinister place
he'll crumple your bones in his bogey embrace.
Never never go near if you hold your life dear,
for oh! . . . what he'll do . . . when he gets you!

THE VAMPIRE

The night is still and somber,
and in the murky gloom,
arisen from his slumber,
the vampire leaves his tomb.

His eyes are pools of fire,
his skin is icy white,
and blood his one desire
this woebegotten night.

Then through the silent city
he makes his silent way,
prepared to take no pity
upon his hapless prey.

An open window beckons,
he grins a hungry grin,
and pausing not one second
he swiftly climbs within.

And there, beneath her covers,
his victim lies in sleep.
With fangs agleam, he hovers
and with those fangs, bites deep.

The vampire drinks till sated,
he fills his every pore,
and then, his thirst abated,
licks clean the dripping gore.

With powers now replenished,
his thirst no longer burns.
His quest this night is finished,
so to his tomb he turns,

and there awhile in silence
he'll rest beneath the mud
until, with thoughts of violence,
he wakes and utters . . . blood!

THE DRAGON OF DEATH

In a faraway, faraway forest
lies a treasure of infinite worth,
but guarding it closely forever
looms a being as old as the earth.

Its body is big as a boulder
and armored with shimmering scales,
even the mountaintops tremble
when it thrashes its seven great tails.

Its eyes tell a story of terror,
they gleam with an angry red flame
as it timelessly watches its riches,
and the dragon of death is its name.

Its teeth are far sharper than daggers,
they can tear hardest metal to shreds.
It has seven mouths filled with these weapons,
for its neck swells to seven great heads.

Each head is as fierce as the other,
Each head breathes a fiery breath,
and any it touches must perish,
set ablaze by the dragon of death.

All who have foolishly stumbled
on the dragon of death's golden cache
remain evermore in that forest,
nothing left of their bodies but ash.

THE TROLL

Be wary of the loathsome troll
that slyly lies in wait
to drag you to his dingy hole
and put you on his plate.

His blood is black and boiling hot,
he gurgles ghastly groans.
He'll cook you in his dinner pot,
your skin, your flesh, your bones.

He'll catch your arms and clutch your legs
and grind you to a pulp,
then swallow you like scrambled eggs—
gobble! gobble! gulp!

So watch your steps when next you go
upon a pleasant stroll,
or you might end in the pit below
as supper for the troll.

THE WITCH

She comes by night, in fearsome flight,
   in garments black as pitch,
the queen of doom upon her broom,
   the wild and wicked witch,

a cackling crone with brittle bones
   and desiccated limbs,
two evil eyes with warts and sties
   and bags about the rims,

a dangling nose, ten twisted toes
   and folds of shriveled skin,
cracked and chipped and crackled lips
   that frame a toothless grin.

She hurtles by, she sweeps the sky
   and hurls a piercing screech.
As she swoops past, a spell is cast
   on all her curses reach.

Take care to hide when the wild witch rides
   to shriek her evil spell.
What she may do with a word or two
   is much too grim to tell.

THE OGRE

In a foul and filthy cavern
where the sun has never shone,
the one-eyed ogre calmly gnaws
a cold and moldy bone.

He sits in silence in the slime
that fills his fetid home
and notes the nearing footsteps
in the monstrous catacomb.

The one-eyed ogre drools with joy,
his stony heart beats fast,
he knows that for some girl or boy
this day shall be their last.

He wields his ugly cudgel
in a wide and vicious arc,
it swiftly finds his victim
in the deep and deadly dark.

Then down and down and down again
the ogre's blows descend,
to rend, and render senseless,
to speed his victim's end.

So pity those who stumble through
the one-eyed ogre's cave—
that dark abode he calls his home
shall surely be their grave.

THE WEREWOLF

The full moon glows, foreboding,
and I quake from head to feet
for this night I know, in the town below,
the werewolf prowls the street.

He stalks with stealth and cunning
in his search for a soul to eat.
With matted hair and jaws that tear,
the werewolf prowls the street.

His face is filled with fury
as his brain cries out for meat,
and oh his prey shall not see day
for the werewolf prowls the street.

So I shake beneath my covers
and I shiver in my sheet
and I cower in my bed with a pillow on my head,
as the werewolf prowls the street.

THE WIZARD

The wizard, watchful, waits alone
within his tower of cold gray stone
and ponders in his wicked way
what evil deeds he'll do this day.
He's tall and thin, with wrinkled skin,
a tangled beard hangs from his chin,
his cheeks are gaunt, his eyes set deep,
he scarcely eats, he needs no sleep.

       His fingers wave arcane commands,
       ten bony sticks on withered hands,
       his flowing cloak is smirched with grime,
       he's worn it since the dawn of time.
       Upon his hat, in silver lines
       are pictured necromantic signs,
       symbols of the awesome power
       of the wizard, alone in his cold stone tower.

He scans his mystic stock in trade—
charms to fetch a demon's aid,
seething stews of purplish potions,
throbbing thaumaturgic lotions,
supernatural tracts and tomes
replete with lore of elves and gnomes,
talismans, amulets, willowy wand
to summon spirits from beyond.

He spies a bullfrog by the door
and stooping, scoops it off the floor.
He flicks his wand, the frog's a flea
through elemental sorcery,
the flea hops once, the flea hops twice,
the flea becomes a pair of mice
that dive into a bubbling brew,
emerging as one cockatoo.

      The wizard laughs a hollow laugh,
      the soaking bird's reduced by half,
      and when, perplexed, it starts to squawk,
      the wizard turns it into chalk
      with which he deftly writes a spell
      that makes the chalk a silver bell
      which tinkles in the ashen air
      till flash . . . a fire burns brightly there.

He gestures with an ancient knack
to try to bring the bullfrog back.
Another flash! . . . no flame now burns
as once again the frog returns,
but when it bounds about in fear,
the wizard shouts, "Begone from here,"
and midway through a frightened croak
it vanishes in clouds of smoke.

      The wizard smirks a fiendish smirk
      reflecting on the woes he'll work
      as he consults a dusty text
      and checks which hex he'll conjure next.
      He may pluck someone off the spot
      and turn him into . . . who knows what?
      Should you encounter a toad or lizard,
      look closely . . . it may be the work of the wizard.

THE GHOUL

The gruesome ghoul, the grisly ghoul,
   without the slightest noise
waits patiently beside the school
to feast on girls and boys.

He lunges fiercely through the air
as they come out to play,
then grabs a couple by the hair
and drags them far away.

He cracks their bones and snaps their backs
and squeezes out their lungs,
he chews their thumbs like candy snacks
and pulls apart their tongues.

He slices their stomachs and bites their hearts
and tears their flesh to shreds,
he swallows their toes like toasted tarts
and gobbles down their heads.

Fingers, elbows, hands and knees
and arms and legs and feet—
he eats them with delight and ease,
for every part's a treat.

And when the gruesome, grisly ghoul
has nothing left to chew,
he hurries to another school
and waits . . . perhaps for you.

THE DANCE OF THE THIRTEEN SKELETONS

In a snow-enshrouded graveyard
gripped by winter's bitter chill,
not a single soul is stirring,
all is silent, all is still
till a distant bell tolls midnight
and the spirits work their will.

For emerging from their coffins
buried deep beneath the snow,
thirteen bony apparitions
now commence their spectral show,
and they gather in the moonlight
undulating as they go.

      And they'll dance in their bones,
      in their bare bare bones,
      with the click and the clack
      and the chitter and the chack
      and the clatter and the chatter
      of their bare bare bones.

They shake their flimsy shoulders
and they flex their fleshless knees
and they nod their skulls in greeting
in the penetrating breeze
as they form an eerie circle
near the gnarled and twisted trees.

They link their spindly fingers
as they promenade around
casting otherworldly shadows
on the silver-mantled ground
and their footfalls in the snowdrift
make a soft, susurrous sound.

      And they dance in their bones,
      in their bare bare bones,
      with the click and the clack
      and the chitter and the chack
      and the clatter and the chatter
      of their bare bare bones.

The thirteen grinning skeletons
continue on their way
as to strains of soundless music
they begin to swing and sway
and they circle ever faster
in their ghastly roundelay.

Faster, faster ever faster
and yet faster now they race,
winding, whirling, ever swirling
in the frenzy of their pace
and they shimmer in the moonlight
as they spin themselves through space.

And they dance in their bones,
in their bare bare bones,
with the click and the clack
and the chitter and the chack
and the clatter and the chatter
of their bare bare bones.

Then as quickly as it started
their nocturnal dance is done
for the bell that is their signal
loudly tolls the hour of one
and they bow to one another
in their bony unison.

Then they vanish to their coffins
by their ghostly thoroughfare
and the emptiness of silence
once more fills the frosted air
and the snows that mask their footprints
show no sign that they were there.

But they danced in their bones,
in their bare bare bones,
with the click and the clack
and the chitter and the chack
and the clatter and the chatter
of their bare bare bones.